W9-BDW-295

What will I write?

Bobbie Kalman
Crabtree Publishing Company
www.crabtreebooks.com

Created by Bobbie Kalman

Dedicated by Julie Love, for Benjamin,
Our future race car driver and Maxwell, Benjamin's #1 fan!
Mommy and Daddy love you very much xoxo

Author
Bobbie Kalman

Editor
Kathy Middleton

Educational consultants
Jennifer King
Janine Deschenes
Reagan Miller

Photo research
Bobbie Kalman

Design
Bobbie Kalman
Katherine Berti
Samara Parent (cover)

Print coordinator
Katherine Berti

Photographs
Bigstockphoto: Regi: p. 4 (bottom)
Shutterstock: Cassiohabib: p. 15 (left)
Thinkstock: Tom Brakefield p. 13
   (middle), 23 (bottom bears)
Cover and all other images
   by Shutterstock

Library and Archives Canada Cataloguing in Publication

Kalman, Bobbie, author
   What will I write? / Bobbie Kalman.

(My world)
Includes index.
Issued in print and electronic formats.
ISBN 978-0-7787-9600-8 (hardcover).
ISBN 978-0-7787-9608-4 (softcover).
ISBN 978-1-4271-1981-0 (HTML)

    1. Composition (Language arts)--Juvenile literature.
2. Writing--Juvenile literature. 3. Literature--Terminology--Juvenile
literature. 4. English language--Composition and exercises--Juvenile
literature. 5. English language--Writing--Juvenile literature.
6. English language--Terminology--Juvenile literature.
I. Title. II. Series: My world (St. Catharines, Ont.)

LB1576.K35 2017   j372.62'3   C2017-905178-4
                                             C2017-905179-2

Library of Congress Cataloging-in-Publication Data

Names: Kalman, Bobbie, author.
Title: What will I write? / Bobbie Kalman.
Description: New York, New York : Crabtree Publishing Company, (2018) |
   Series: My world | Includes index.
Identifiers: LCCN 2017051018 (print) | LCCN 2017059293 (ebook) |
   ISBN 9781427119810 (Electronic HTML) |
   ISBN 9780778796008 (reinforced library binding) |
   ISBN 9780778796084 (pbk.)
Subjects: LCSH: Authorship--Juvenile literature. | Creative writing--
   Juvenile literature.
Classification: LCC PN159 (ebook) | LCC PN159 .K35 2018 (print) |
   DDC 372.62/3--dc23
LC record available at https://lccn.loc.gov/2017051018

Crabtree Publishing Company
www.crabtreebooks.com   1-800-387-7650

Printed in the U.S.A./022018/CG20171220

Published in Canada
Crabtree Publishing
616 Welland Ave.
St. Catharines, Ontario
L2M 5V6

Published in the United States
Crabtree Publishing
PMB 59051
350 Fifth Avenue, 59th Floor
New York, New York 10118

Published in the United Kingdom
Crabtree Publishing
Maritime House
Basin Road North, Hove
BN41 1WR

Published in Australia
Crabtree Publishing
3 Charles Street
Coburg North
VIC 3058

Contents

Information or story?

Nonfiction writing often shows readers information through photographs like these.

Do you like to read to learn new things, or do you prefer to read for fun? Different kinds of writing are used to tell a story or give information.

Nonfiction

Text, or writing, that contains facts about our world is called **nonfiction**. It gives us information about people, animals, history, countries, sports, and many other subjects.

4

Fiction

Fiction is writing created by the imagination, such as this fairy tale. It is not true, but it can be based on real facts or people. Many books, movies, and TV shows are fiction.

Pictures help make text easier to understand. What part of the "The Three Little Pigs" fairy tale do you think this picture shows?

Pictures and words

Nonfiction writing gives facts about a subject. **Headings** and **captions** are used to organize the information on the page. A heading is like a title that tells what the writing below it is about. What is the heading on this page? Captions give information about pictures. Nonfiction writing often has **diagrams**, too, like the one on page 7.

*This caption tells that a baby deer, called a **fawn**, is sniffing one of the two baby skunks in the picture. What do you think the fawn will do if the skunk sprays it?*

A butterfly diagram

A diagram uses pictures and words to show or explain something. This diagram shows how a butterfly changes from an egg to an adult.

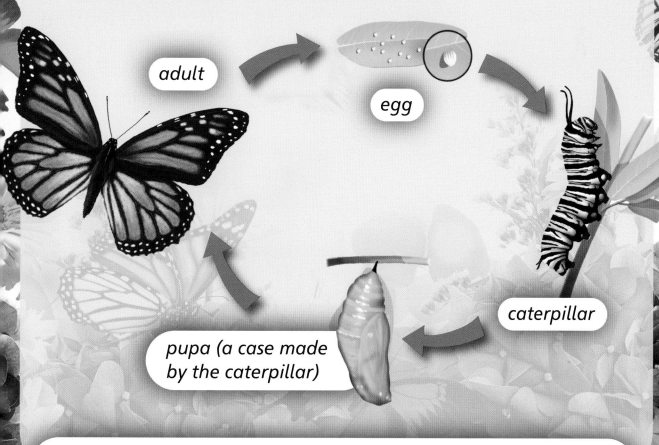

adult

egg

caterpillar

pupa (a case made by the caterpillar)

Look at the diagram and write in sentences the changes a butterfly goes through. Use words such as first, next, then, and finally.

Words that describe

Writers try to create a picture of a subject in the reader's mind. To do this, they give details and use words that describe what the reader might see, smell, hear, taste, or touch, using their **five senses**. Text that describes is used in both fiction and nonfiction writing.

octopus

polar bear

giraffes

camel

frog

skunk

Adjectives describe

Words that describe a person, place, or thing are called **adjectives**. Choose some of the adjectives in this box to write a story, poem, or song to describe the animals on these pages.

tall, heavy, big, tiny, small, pink, brown, green, yellow, black, striped, bumpy, stinky, wavy, shiny, slimy, long, jumpy, white, spotted, furry, smooth, young, colorful, blind, hairy

worm

fish

baby rats

Can you find these animals?

Which animal is tall? Which ones are small?
Which are green, brown, or pinky?
Which one can smell really stinky?
Which look wavy, spotted, or bumpy?
Which is slimy, striped, or jumpy?
Which has fur that is mostly white?
Which ones are heavy, and which are light?

Writing styles

Writing is used to explain or describe something to a reader or to answer questions. Writers use different **styles**, or types, of text for different reasons.

- To tell a story, which can be fiction or nonfiction
- To give information about a subject
- To give an **opinion** about something and the reasons why they feel that way
- To describe something using details and the five senses

With a reading partner, find examples of different writing styles used in this book.

in my opinion   my favorite

I think   I prefer

I feel   I believe

                            I disagree

An opinion is what you believe about a subject. Writers use words such as these to give their opinions.

This girl is reading a story she wrote.

This teacher is helping his students write information about animals.

I smell
I taste
I feel
I hear
I see

This girl is showing pictures and writing words that describe the five senses.

These students are writing a poem about why they feel that butterflies are an important part of nature!

Setting, characters, plot

A story is made up of events that take place. Stories can be fiction or nonfiction. Every story has a beginning, middle, and an end. It includes a **setting**, which is where the story takes place, **characters**, and a **plot**. The plot describes the main events that take place in a story.

A polar bear family

These pages tell a nonfiction story about a polar bear family. The main characters are a mother bear and her two **cubs**, or babies. The setting of the story is a cold place called the Arctic. Polar bears live in the Arctic, which is at the very top of Earth.

The cubs are born in a deep hole in the snow called a den. They must soon leave the den so their mother can teach them how to hunt.

Read the story in the captions next to the photos. The plot of the story is what happens to the cubs. After they are born, they go on a long walk to the ocean, where they learn how to hunt. With a reading partner, retell how the story begins, what happens in the middle, and how it ends.

The cubs follow their mother to the ocean to hunt seals. To hunt, the cubs will need to learn how to jump from one sheet of ice to another and how to swim in the ocean.

When they reach the ocean, the mother teaches her cubs to smell for seals under the ice. They wait for a seal to poke its nose out of the water to get air. When it does, the mother bear grabs it!

13

Write your story!

Everyone has fascinating stories to tell! Think about happy, exciting, or sad events that have happened to you. You can turn these into stories about your life. Make a list of the things you want to include in your story, such as your memories, feelings, and any opinions you want to share. Will your ending make your readers remember your story?

1 What events take place in your story?

2 Who are the characters?

3 Use your five senses to describe where and when it happened.

4 Describe your thoughts and feelings using adjectives.

5 How will your story end?

My vacation story

Use details to describe a vacation. Make sure your story has a beginning, middle, and an end.

- Who went with you?
- Where did you go?
- How did you get there?
- What did you see?
- Why was the vacation fun?

Write a story about a special vacation you took to celebrate your family's culture.

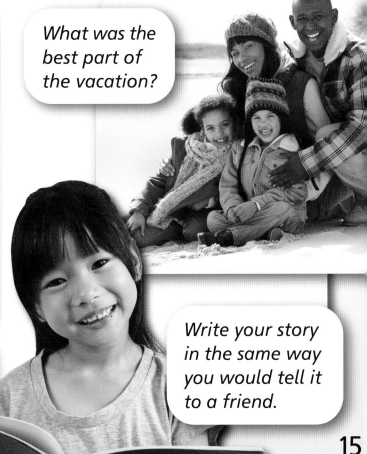

What was the best part of the vacation?

Write your story in the same way you would tell it to a friend.

Fun with fiction

Writing fiction is fun because you can be creative and tell a story using your imagination. You could retell a true story and change the characters, setting, and ending. You could also make up the entire story yourself.

Use these writing tips

1. Decide on the characters and the setting.
2. Start with a funny, exciting, or scary sentence to get readers interested right away.
3. Give your characters a problem or mystery to solve or write a funny plot for them.
4. Have your characters show their feelings.
5. Make yourself part of the story.
6. Write an ending that will make your readers think about what you have shared with them.

What will I write?

- If everyone in my family was a superhero, what super powers would each person have?
- Would we be able to fly, lift heavy things, have super vision, be able to climb high mountains, or speak many languages?
- How could we help other people?
- What would you do if you had super powers?

Getting creative

It doesn't matter whether you write a story, poem, or song. Being creative is the most important part of writing. Here are some fun ideas for you to try.

With some friends, write a song about your school and perform the song for your classmates.

Take a story you know, like "Little Red Riding Hood," and change parts of it to make a new story.

- How could you make yourself part of the story?
- How might you change the ending?

Pretend you are a king or queen in a fairy tale. What laws would you create to make people happy?

19

Create a project!

Do you like learning about animals, art, countries, or machines? You can learn a lot about a subject if you do a project about it. Find some partners to help you. Decide what subject you want to research. Make a list of questions that you want to answer about the subject. The questions can be your **contents** list, like the one on page 3 of this book.

Brainstorm, or discuss ideas, with your partners. Then ask your teacher for more ideas about your project.

Brainstorm

Make a plan!

- Decide which questions each partner will research.
- Each page should have both information and artwork.
- Find your information in library books or on a computer. Ask an adult for help.

Did you include...?

- ✓ a contents list
- ✓ headings
- ✓ diagrams
- ✓ captions
- ✓ a cover

Draw pictures to help show the information in your project.

Our Project

Writing your opinions

Writing your opinions means saying what you think, feel, or believe about something and giving reasons why.

My opinions count!

Pretend your family wants to get a pet. Give your opinion on which kind of animal would make the best pet. Think of some of the good points and bad points of owning and caring for different pets. End with a sentence that says why you finally chose the pet you did.

Do you prefer an animal that you can run around with outdoors or one that stays indoors?

Would you prefer to clean a litter box or take your pet for a walk?

Do you believe that everyone in your family should get his or her own pet?

Words to know and Index

Objectives
- To teach children some of the features of fiction and nonfiction writing
- To introduce children to different kinds of writing for different purposes
- To teach children the different parts of a story

Before Reading
- Read the title to the children and ask them what they think the book will be about.
- Scan the Contents list and discuss what they may learn from the book.
- Give children sticky notes to jot down a few key words after they read each section.

During Reading
- Ask the children how pictures, photos, and diagrams help them understand the text. How are the pictures used in nonfiction writing different from those used in fiction?
- Ask the children to write five adjectives that describe themselves.

After Reading
- Ask the children to identify the nonfiction text features in this book. Invite them to share how those features help them learn.
- Ask the children to name the different styles of writing they learned about in this book.
- Ask them to share their favorite book and describe which text features it has to support their understanding.

Put it in Order!
Invite the children to write a story with a beginning, middle, and end. Prompt them to use the words first, next, then, and finally. Have the children put their story out of order, switch their jumbled stories with a partner, and then put each other's story back in its correct order.

Use your Senses!
Ask the children to choose an object in the classroom and write a description of it that uses the five senses. Invite children to share their description. Ask them to identify each sense in their writing.

Be a Writing Expert!
Invite the children to revisit the writing tips on page 16. Ask them to brainstorm more tips that they would use for fiction as well as nonfiction writing.

More Information
The book about polar bears below tells the whole story of the polar bear family on pages 12–13. Read this book, as well as the other animal family adventure books, to the children and ask them to write fiction or nonfiction stories about animals, based on the books.